Your Family Tree

Text: **Núria Roca**

Illustrations: **Rosa M. Curto**

Look at this fantastic tree! It is a special tree, because real trees do not have names or pictures hanging from them.

This is Martin's family tree. You can see all the
people in his family and some of his ancestors.

Ancestors are those people in your family who were born before you were: your grandparents, your great-grandparents, your great-great-grandparents…

They are very special people because they are part of your life and your past history.

Martin's paternal grandfather, that is, his dad's father, came from Japan when he was young. A few months after his arrival he met Grandmother Margaret. They liked each other so much that they got married.

They had three children: Aunt Helen, Uncle Paul, and Martin's dad.

Martin's maternal grandparents (his mom's parents) also met when they were young. Grandma was a baker and Grandpa was a fireman. One day there was a fire in the bakery…and they fell in love!

Grandma died a year ago, and Martin still remembers her and feels very sad. He loved her so much!

In the tree you can also see Martin's great-grandparents,
who were his grandparents' parents. Martin's great-
grandparents died many years before he was born,
but his parents have shown him pictures of them.
Martin loves to hear stories about his great-grandparents.
Do you know any story about your own great-
grandparents?

Your grandparents' parents are your great-grandparents and your great-grandparents' parents are…your great-great-grandparents! Grandparents, great-grandparents, great-great-grandparents… We can go on like this until we reach your most distant relatives. You have a lot of ancestors!

In Martin's family tree there is
no room for all of his ancestors;
that's why he has drawn a tree
with just his present family: his
grandparents, his parents, and
his brother and sister.
A brother and a sister on each
side of the tree and Martin right
in the middle of the trunk!

Martin laughs the same way his mother does, and his eyes and way of walking are like his father's. But he is very untidy, and in this aspect he does not take after his mom or dad.

Do you look like your parents? Do you take after them? And after your grandparents?

In some aspects we resemble our parents, but not in everything!

Martin finds he is like his sister in that they are both full of mischief and like his brother in that they are both absentminded. But the shape of their faces and the color of their hair are quite different.

When they come back from
the playground, the three of
them are so dirty they all look
the same.

Your parents' brothers and sisters are your uncles and aunts. Martin has three uncles and two aunts. He often sees two of them, but the other three live very far away.

Do your parents have brothers and sisters? Are they older or younger than your mom and dad?

Martin gets along very well with his dad's kid brother. His uncle married a girl from Ecuador, who is now Martin's aunt. They are going to have a baby soon, and it will be Martin's youngest cousin. His aunt and uncle love dancing. They are Martin's favorite!

Martin has a lot of cousins. He shares the same family name with some of them, but not with others. Do you know why?

That's because some of his cousins come from his father's side of the family, while the rest come from his mother's side. They are all his cousins just the same, but not all of them have the same last name.

Martin has a cousin who is afraid of dogs, another cousin who is blind and is crazy about music, a red-headed cousin who wants to be an astronaut, and even one little cousin who still wets his diapers…
What are your cousins like?

We talk about a family tree because your family is like a tree with many branches from which all your relatives' names hang.

If we put together all the family trees belonging to your friends at school we would not have a tree but a whole forest!

A very special tree

This is your family tree! You only need to trace it on a piece of cardboard and then glue pictures of your parents, brothers, sisters, as well as your own. If you have no pictures, then you may draw everybody and the result will be just as great.

Looking for everybody's pictures is great fun!

My family's book

There are many, many things you may cut out!

The tree is very nice, but it is small and there are many people missing from it, such as uncles and aunts, cousins, and other relatives. How about making a book where all your relatives are included? You just need some sheets of paper, old magazines, family pictures, and your parents to tell you stories about the family members. Let's begin with your grandparents. First, get a picture of your maternal grandfather, glue it to a piece of paper, and then you and your parents start going over some magazines looking for things related to your grandpa. For example, a rose because he likes plants, a light-bulb because he used to be an electrician, a very tall building because he was born in a big city…. There are plenty of things you may cut out from the magazines. When you finish collecting items for your grandpa, start with your maternal grandmother and do the same. Once done, go on with your paternal grandparents, your aunts and uncles, your cousins, your cat…. When you have everybody, you just need to add a front and back cover made of cardboard, punch two holes on the side and pass a string through so all the sheets of paper will be bound. There, you now have a family album!

Making a picture

Don't forget to name each person.

Get a piece of thick cardboard, close your eyes, and imagine all your family. Who will you draw first? When you have completed the drawing of the first relative, start with the next and don't forget any of them! You may use color pencils, markers, watercolors, or pieces of color tissue paper to make the clothes they are wearing, their hair, shoes, and so on. When you are done, you may hang the picture in your bedroom or take it with you to the next family reunion so everybody can see how well they look.

A tree with dangling pictures

Now that you know how to draw your family tree, how about turning it into a sculpture? All you need is some easy-to-bend wire, strips of tissue paper, and pictures of your grandparents, your mom and dad, your brothers and sisters, and one picture of yourself.

Ask a grownup to cut six pieces of wire. Bend each at the middle and twist both halves a bit. Then get all six wires together, twist them at the bottom to form the trunk of the tree. Twist the strands to form the branches, as the illustration shows. The tree will stand if you stick the six ends twisted together in a base made of plasticine or clay. When you complete this, wrap thin strips of tissue paper around the branches; use some paper glue to keep them in place. The tree is ready. Now you only need to hang the pictures from the branches using paper clips. Your grandparents' pictures go at the very top, then your parents a little bit lower, and you and your brothers and sisters, if you have them, go in the lowest branches.

It is a very artistic tree!

Note to parents

The family tree

The tree introduced in the activities is simple, and therefore adequate for very young children. If your children wish to make a more complex and interesting tree, you may attempt one that is taller and has more branches, and place the maternal and paternal grandparents at the very top. This will require looking for more pictures or making additional drawings. If no pictures are available, you may help the children by telling them what their grandparents were like: the color of their eyes and their hair, the hairstyles they favored, the clothes they used to wear, their heights and shapes… As the tree is being built, the children will realize that it gets more and more complicated as you add ancestors.

A family book

A good way to describe the relatives that surround the child is looking for illustrations that remind us of them. Sometimes, when we are writing, we focus on some characteristics and do not realize we leave out many others. But when we look for pictures in an old magazine and relate them to the person, we pay attention to details that we might not have considered otherwise.
The album can be made as indicated in the description of the activity or by going through the magazine and cutting out whatever reminds us of some family member. Pool all the clippings together. When you are done, supervise the child as he or she chooses the clippings that correspond to the person involved and glues them in place. This is a good way to exercise the memory.

Making a tree

For the tree-making activity you may look at all the pictures you have where parents, grandparents, brothers and sisters, aunts and uncles appear. While you are looking at the pictures, you may recall things that happened the day the picture was taken or other aspects related to the family member you are talking about. Most probably, the kids will soon feel like talking about situations or events they link with that person. If they did not get to meet their grandparents or great-grandparents, you may portray them as the children's ancestors and describe their circumstances. It is important to mention all the experiences grandparents have accumulated in their lives and, most of all, it is important to talk about them with great respect. It is essential that children learn at an early age how to respect others, and the family is the right start.

Relationships

Explain what it means when you say paternal or maternal grandparents. Tell them that paternal grandparents are their father's parents, and maternal grandparents are their mother's parents. Most probably, the children will want to hear how each family lived then, the differences and similarities with the present, and what life was like when they were two separate families.

The pictures on this page may help you answer some questions about family relationships, which are hard to understand when they go back several generations. Obviously, you should adjust your explanations to the age of the children.

YOUR FAMILY TREE

First edition for the United States and Canada
published in 2007 by Barron's Educational Series,
Inc.
© Copyright 2006 by Gemser Publications, S.L.
C/Castell, 38; Teià (08329) Barcelona, Spain
(World Rights)

Author: Núria Roca
Illustrator: Rosa M. Curto

All inquiries should be addressed to:
Barron's Educational Series, Inc.
250 Wireless Boulevard
Hauppauge, New York, 11788
http://www.barronseduc.com

ISBN-13: 978-0-7641-3579-8
ISBN-10: 0-7641-3579-1
Library of Congress Control Number 2006931049

Printed in China
9 8 7 6 5 4 3 2 1